Carl Nielsen

THE CHILDREN ARE PLAYING

Flute Solo

WH

EDITION WILHELM HANSEN AS

Børnene spiller

The Children are Playing — Die Kinder spielen

FLAUTO SOLO

Carl Nielsen

*) Hele stykket kan repeteres herfra.
The whole piece may be repeated from here.
Das ganze Stück kann von hier repetiert werden.

27818